Papa's Rhyme Without Reason

Poems; Short Verses and One-Liners

by

John D. Schmitz

Dorrance Publishing Co
585 Alpha Drive
Pittsburgh, PA 15238
Visit our website at www.dorrancebookstore.com

ISBN: 979-8-88812-161-0
eISBN: 979-8-88812-661-5

Introduction

The contents of this book contain pages of poetry dedicated to the praise and glory of the Lord and man's lifelong quest for eternal life, as well as pages on life, love, and Mother Nature.

About the Author

I have always enjoyed writing poetry over the years. It has allowed me to express my thoughts through words on a variety of topics for all to read. Through my university education, and my life's long work in gardening and landscaping, creativity through imagination has always played a part in that to which I wrote and will continue to write.

Preface

Poems, short verses, and one-liners

by John D. Schmitz

(with heartfelt love and thanks to my late wife Darcy A. Schmitz)

Table of Contents

"Reflections"

The sun shines brightly through the skies of blue

Touching the highest mountain tops with her radiant rays

Warming the waters and land far below

Illuminating with light where darkness now sleeps

The dawning of a new day is with us once again

A time to reflect upon all that there is

With an open heart and mind, I shall seek

To be with the Creator of all that I see

In heaven with the Lord, for all eternity

The Lord's love and kindness engulfs all of mankind

The choosing is yours to the ending of time.

"Giant Sequoia"

The sun's rays barely reach the forest floor, far, far below

As these giants stand aloft, like soldiers guarding their sole domain

Branches like huge arms, stretching out across miles and miles

Massive trunks lay anchored within the forest's walls hidden treasurers

Life there is protected by centuries of Mother Nature's rule

Forgotten in the passage of time

Giants among giants in the eye of one who beholds

Relics of time, reaching upwards toward the heavenly skies

A marvel created by "the Lord" and watched over through the eyes of
"Mother Nature"

Almighty King

Trees swaying about in the cool breezes

With leaves that seem to decorate the autumn sky

While the ground everywhere becomes covered by a quilt of many colors

Until the next gust of wind blows them about to their new destination

Yes; fall is truly the gateway for "Mother Nature"

Which then opens the doorway to a white wintery

Wonderland

Where many, many years ago

A star shone brightly upon a stable

Where in the manger a child lies

A King of Kings whose throne is not of earthly domain

As Heaven's Angels sing His glorious praise

Glory To Him In The Highest

And peace To His People On Earth

JOHN D. SCHMITZ

Northland

The waters glisten in the evening sun

Surrounded by trees and the sounds of "Mother Nature"

Wisconsin's northland is laid to rest

Amidst the twinkling of stars

And the moon's faint shadow

Voices afar and the scattering of lights

Slowly fade to nature's beckon call

As the carpet of darkness has

Blanketed the nighttime sky

Awakening only to the dawning of a new day

Good Night To All And To All A Good night

"My Heart"

I ponder about many yesterdays

Of dreams that hopefully come true

For in my heart I'll always have

A special place for you

The Lord has taken you to eternity's rest

Beyond the skies of blue

Someday I hope to join you there

Be it the blessings of the Lord come true

CAUSES

Wear a shirt; take a knee;

walk upon this very land

Justice for all or all for justice

It's time we take a stand

Those flames of inequality

light up the evening sky

with the hope of notoriety

that will surely catch one's eye

Change is on the front burner

On the back burner shall it stay

The realities of many a poor folk

who didn't march today

So give of time, effort or cause;

money if you can

for all the races, sexes, and

creeds that grace this very land

TIME

Time waits for no one;

and no one waits for time

It can get quite confusing

when these words are put to rhyme

Yes meaning has its beginnings

and so too has its ends

to which you'll have to figure out

to fully comprehend

Those wheels of thought; they slowly turn

in each and everyone

Within the minds of all of us

this process has begun

To the past, present, and future

Without time there wouldn't be a thought

or word: spoken or heard from

now to eternity

JOHN D. SCHMITZ

MIRROR OF LIFE

The mirror of life has many reflections

illuminating both you and I

Look shall you see; whatever there shall be

as "Mother Nature" and time say goodbye

To the past shall you look

Now the present is here

To the future you must now hold on

for these mirrors shine so bright

within our memory's hindsight

showing those pathways

that are already gone

THE DOOR OF LIFE

The door of life is always open

So take a look you'll see

those marvels that are within one's self

touched up by reality

There are doors that open up so wide

while others close so tight

This door that is within yourself

is open day and night.

So say a little prayer my friend

It will bring you peace of mind

For within thyself

you'll surely see

that love you're searching to find

JOHN D. SCHMITZ

PAPA'S TUNES

Shall all my poems contain

rhyme, rhythm, and harmony

Perhaps leave that all to music

where it really ought to be

True words not of simplistic meaning

surely you can comprehend

only reaching to that final point

where beginning is the end

To start is not to finish

On paper do I write

a tune of many melodies

which brightens up my life

QUESTION?

Does a word have a meaning

or a meaning have a word

Is everything you hear

all that you have heard

Answer thus this question

In the minds of many men

it wills to paradoxity

to which there is no end

Is man's finite nature

his true reality

to which there was

to which there is

to which we'll have to see

?

JOHN D. SCHMITZ

LIFE'S ROAD

Life's past is just a memory

in the presence of today

The future is what is coming

for each and every day

for this road that we all travel on

with its many twists and turns

The end is coming soon my friend

and we all shall take our turn

So remember this thy hearty soul

of things you cannot see

A weary heart has found its home

in Heaven for eternity

SLEEP

To sleep or not to sleep

So simple would it seem

Gently lay thy head to rest

and fill it full of dreams

"JOHN"

l don't need sleep;

I have to finish this task that is at hand

I'll get some later if time permits

Surely you can understand

"DARCY"

I understand that sleep's important

for each and every one so upon

this pillow your head to rest

your dreaming has begun

JOHN D. SCHMITZ

HAPPINESS

When reflecting on life's moments

sit down and crack a smile

Pour yourself a cool one

You may be here for a while

Close your eyes and let your mind

wander off to sleep

It's there that you'll find memories

In your lifetime shall you keep

when you awake from slumber's rest

On your face there's still a grin

over a lifetime full of memories

and this empty glass of gin

DARCY

She gave when there was little left to give

and yet she found still more

Her love was always open for us

She'll never close that door

She was a wife and mother

throughout the years

that all of us have known

But to me she stood like a fortress strong

in my heart I call my home

I thank her for the tears she shed

when things weren't always right

I thank her for the smile she had

that brightened up our lives

but most of all I am thankful for

the true love she left behind

a legacy left in my heart

and always in my mind

JOHN D. SCHMITZ

LIFE

Life is not a science

created in a tube

It comes from God's creation

within a mother's womb

Science takes its place

in the minds of many men

The Lord has all creation

from the beginning to the end

Thank the scientific world

for the good that they have done

Raise your heads to the heavens above

where their enlightenment all came from

DARCY'S PLACE

She rests upon the angel's wing

A better place she'll be

where happiness and joy abound

and love flows endlessly

Her worldly troubles are left behind

and His arms are open wide

The Lord is standing at Heaven's gate

with Darcy at His side

"Love John"

JOHN D. SCHMITZ

FAMILY

A family has different meanings
to folks you're going to find
Some are happy; others sad;
some say never mind
When I sit down and think about
throughout those many years
my family that stood by me
through sadness, joy, and tears
they always gave, but seldom took
That's the way they'll always be
May God's loving hands extend to
them and blessed shall they be.

NEW LIFE

Looking back in the rear-view mirror

of life at all that could have been done

Second guessing the past; in your

memory will last

while the future has already begun

Change what you can or will

what you change

and the rest of life leave it alone

For the sake of yourself you surely can

see that the past and the future are one

So close those tired eyes; open up your heart

let the past and the future come in

When you thus awake some

changes shall you make

This new life you are ready to begin

FRIENDS

Friends are sincere in thought and word

giving advice you hopefully heard

Call them up and talk a while

They'll always go that extra mile

Friends of mine go back in time

many years ago and hard to find

As "Mother Nature" slowly passes by

I'll still let out a joyful sigh

Those memories in my mind that play

of those good friends I have today

May the Lord look down upon all of them

with His blessing that will never end

LOVE

The worries of tomorrow
caught up in those today
are but a fleeting memory
to a little girl at play
Those happy-go-lucky feelings
secured within her heart
knowing nothing would ever
enter there
that could tear them all apart
Daddy stands a vigilant watch
over his daughter every day
so that happiness and love persist
for that little girl at play

A PRAYER

A prayer could be an omen

of things that are to come

Thankfulness or forgiveness

when all is said and done

A prayer transcends the mind

when spoken from the heart

Raise thy head up to the heavens

That's where a prayer will start

The Father, Son, and Holy Spirit

The Blessed Trinity

Our Father and Hail Mary

and glory shall there be

REALITY

Emotions fill the hearts of men

from beginning to the end

Reality is but one of them

to which we all depend

Our lives have different realities

from which you'll build upon

Some you choose; others you don't

as time in life moves on

Experience is the best teacher

that you will come to see

for within yourself you're going to

find your own realities

JOHN D. SCHMITZ

GOODBYE

With a teary eye and heavy heart

when the time has finally come

the opening of new horizons

and the ones where I came from

The future holds such hopefulness

for there dawns another day

The Lord has guided me through

all of this.

His blessings have shown me the way

The new and old are blended together

in a mix of harmony

When the batch is finished

and finally done

a new life is opened to me

THANK YOU

This screen of flux and horror

within my mind does play

one circumstance that changed my life

on one early August day

Fast forwarding to my present state

looking back on all those years

it brought a smile to my face;

sadness, joy, and tears

These emotions run deep within my heart

In my lifetime shall they always stay

Like a beacon of light; on an overcast night

her love has always shown me the way

JOHN D. SCHMITZ

A CHILD'S LOVE

A child's love is close and dear

straight from the heart and so sincere

It warms the room on a wintry day

with a radiant glow that will always stay

A love that gives but never takes

makes believe or hesitates

A smile that is content in love

looked down upon from above

These feelings are both loud and clear

to all of us both far and near

A child's love is like no other

It warms the heart of every mother

PAPA'S GARDEN

Papa's garden is so delightful to see

come spring; summer; then fall

"Old man winter" finally loosened his reins

so the ground can start to thaw

as the ebbs of winter fade from sight

and springtime takes her throne

The chirping of birds; the sun is shining

Papa's garden is not alone

for this garden was built on

the labors of love

Every bag, bucket, and stone

withstanding the harshness

"Mother Nature" has to give this place

I call "my home"

JOHN D. SCHMITZ

YOURSELF

When you give of yourself

in this very special way

those feelings flow deep within

your heart

Neither good times or bad;

happiness or sad

nor even death could tear them apart

She gave to me this endless love

Her life will always live on

in the hearts and minds of all left behind

as a symbol of her love that's never gone

So today I shall write

a poem from my heart

 which transcends all of my memories

To my wife and best friend

until I see you again

Then we'll be together for all eternity

LONELINESS

Those feelings of loneliness; when no one is there

cast out with emptiness, hate, and despair

You're in a world where it comes and it goes

How long it stays; nobody knows

These feelings are a door that won't open wide

Shout out for help; rather look deep inside

In yourself shall you find

these answers you heed

Let time be your guide; and you shall succeed

Never give up on that which seems impossible

For the top of the mountain is always in sight

"Papa"

JOHN D. SCHMITZ

MOTHER NATURE

What beauty there is to behold

Upon one summer day

The flowers and the trees at bloom

children out to play

a walk upon "Mother Nature's" trail

in woods or prairie land

The wonders of it all untold

for all to understand

God's creations big or small

in memory they'll stay

like a walk upon "Mother Nature's" trail

on a beautiful summer day

LITTLE STAR

Let us gaze upon a star

wondering just where you are

High above the world so high

you brighten up the evening sky

Within the hearts of little ones

amazing wonders have begun

Yes twinkle, twinkle, little star

You've touched us all both near and far

The stars are the gateway

to the gates of Heaven

Papa

JOHN D. SCHMITZ

TARA'S HOUSE

A home not built of brick or stone

nor boards put in between

It stands not on foundation blocks

but rather family

For love and caring take the place

of any brick or stone

Two children live here night and day

and call this place their home

In Tara's house their lives together

a real family

where loving and caring

giving and sharing

is the way it's meant to be

DESTINY

This only road for ye to travel

a journey perilously would be

Cross the sun-danced ocean waters

through trees that beckon the blue of sky

within the forests hidden treasure

and endless stretches of prairieland

For nature's clock is slowly ticking

Your time on earth is now at end

This road that layeth beneath your feet

is one in which your life has traveled

and will lead you to your destiny

with God in Heaven for eternity

PRAISE

Eternity beckons "The will of the Lord"

while the finite existence no longer

shall you see

the tumultuous echoes in the sounds

of the night

as silence rests upon that which is said

A fiery end the repentless shall meet

swallowed in ash damnation for thee

For hearts and minds open to His word

The heavenly kingdom be your just reward

For that which is said; and so shall it be

Praise the glory of the Lord

Almighty is He

THE WINDOW OF MY SOUL

A love that now forever yearns

to guide about these endless dreams

The breaking of the heart no more

My searching for eternity

Cross peaceful waters and endless prairies

a path that takes me to myself

I found within the refuge calling

the window of my soul to rest

At last I am joined with peace forever

Upon the wings of an angel I am carried

through the clouded skies of blue

from this earthly domain released

The window of my soul complete

DEATH

Is death life's true beginning

On earth it spells the end

Time has stopped your worldly existence

that will never be again

To the believer life springs eternal

For the rest damnation's your friend

God's loving hands extend to those

Heaven's gates are open again

Your worldly life shall not mark your death

while on earth the time you have spent

in the praise and glory of the Lord our God

and a heart that's full of repent

MOTHER NATURE'S SONG

Waves thrashing upon the evening shores

Birds singing to the tunes of the sea

Fishing boats headed for the dock of the bay

as the sun's faded shadow

faintly glistens the waters far below

A lighthouse guides a weary soul

as the blanket of darkness perpetrates the

evening sky

while the heavens are starstruck

by the twinkling show

"Mother Nature's" eyes are laid to rest

as the heavens sing this glorious song

peace on earth and good will to men

"Goodnight"

JOHN D. SCHMITZ

MAN TAKETH AWAY

The heavens are a blaze by the starstruck sky

while the Lord looks down upon his earthly domain

Lands covered by smoke-filled hate

Rivers flowing with blood-drenched waters

Words spoken in chaotic tongues

Love lays hidden in sanctuaries of rest

Cries for help lay muzzled beneath their

piercing wounds

as darkness is swept away by the dawning

of the sun

So says the Lord

Happy are those who sit at my table

while others wallow in times endless end

THE DIGITAL WORLD OF ELECTRONIC MAN

Ode to a time when things were yet simple

Now complexity shares a front seat with confusion

and innovation went hand and hand with complication

The pushing of a button in your electronic mind

replaces the pen and pencil in a short period of time

as thoughts became words that were seldom ever heard

From the streaming of your electronic phone

in this digital world that surrounds all mankind

your future seems as bright as Einstein's

but some day man's world will turn to darkness

On bended knee the faithful still pray

Tis the end of man's world and eternity beckons

for this is the Lord's judgement day

JOHN D. SCHMITZ

DESTINY SEARCHING

A mind that wanders in memory's heart

searching for that hidden meaning

within the star-gazed yesterdays

The answer thus precludes oneself

and layeth beneath the thought of trust

in which your endless sight shall see

the blissfulness that eternity brings

be it Heaven thus your destiny

GIVING

The moon rests gently on Heaven's chest

surrounded by the star-struck night

Down on earth a child is born; to Mary

and Joseph on Christmas night

So hark the herald angels sing

Silent of the night there be

Peace on earth and good will to men

Immanuel the newborn king

Christmas time is the day of giving

So should every day there be

for in the hearts of all mankind

is this yearning for eternity

JOHN D. SCHMITZ

HOPE SPRINGS ETERNAL

Yet why do I ponder upon that which is gone

filtering through the many pages of time

Blowing are the leaves of yesteryears' thoughts

Dark was the past may then shall it be

but hope springs eternal for those who do seek

Far out of the darkness a faint light will it shine

The past shall you trample under foot that was

known to this new beginning that now opens

for the existence of man

Your starting and finishing are one to behold

Upon the wings of an angel you'll see

that eternity in Heaven is waiting for thee

DARCY'S SONG

Do not cry a tear for me

for I am doing fine

The love we shared throughout the years

stood the test of time

Take care of the ones I left behind

Make sure they'll be all right

I'll say a prayer for all of you

each and every night

I stood by you both night and day

in times of good and bad

We shared many times of happiness

and shared them when were sad

but most of all I stood by you

till death do us part

I'll always have a place for you

deep within my heart

JOHN D. SCHMITZ

BE THANKFUL FOR

Be thankful for the air we breathe

beneath the sky of blue

Be thankful for the sun's bright rays

which melts the morning dew

To mountain ranges high above

the swirling ocean's floor

And the flag that flies in your front yard

that our country men all fought for

I am thankful for this day that comes

be it once in every year

for the giving and sharing

comfort and caring

in those hearts that shed a tear

TRUE LOVE

A thought so spoken of a word so dear

yet meaningless could this be

to the heart and mind that won't comprehend

Reality is theirs to see

For the wayward souls and hearts must seek

the truth to which all must end

As God's loving arms extend to thee

there's hope in your future again

JOHN D. SCHMITZ

THE GLORY OF LIFE

The walkway of life has many directions

Each day one travels a different path

where the realm of certainty becomes measured

by uncertainty

While man's creed becomes his selfish greed

the life that all must yearn to seek

becomes blinded by the evening's darkest night

The joy of happiness becomes muffled by the

sadness of reality

while time ponders what end shall you meet

The Lord our God says blessed are the chosen ones

for theirs is the kingdom of Heaven

Let the rest perish in fiery ash

A THOUGHT

A thought is but a word unspoken

in the mind of one who contemplates

Our choices are the reality of thought

encompassing all the realm of man

Actions are but thoughts in motion

transforming our reality

to those whose thoughtful choice be beckoned

within the life of possibilities

For choice and actions are one in the same

This lifetime will you ponder so

the end result will hopefully be

with God in Heaven for eternity

JOHN D. SCHMITZ

THE LORD SAYS

It is better blinded than to see without

It is better to live without than to live with

It is better to give than expected to be given to

for it is in receiving that you shall be received

It is in helping that helpfulness shall be yours

It is in understanding that you shall be understood

And it is in loving that you shall be loved

for it is in thankfulness that the answer shall be yours

It is in dying that you are born to eternal life

CHOSEN PATHWAYS

The warmth of the sun's radiant rays

slowly dries the dew from the forests far below

as the color of blue seems painted upon the daylight sky

while creatures move in a robust melancholy manner

Birds floating aimlessly upon the warm summer's breezes

Mountaintops reaching to the heavens above

as the echoes of existence emanate from the

valleys far below

Rivers and streams have carved out centuries of "Mother

Nature's" plan

As for myself; I will sit down and evaluate

all that there was; all that there is; and all that

there could be

along God's pathway through life

JOHN D. SCHMITZ

LITTLE ONE'S PRAYER

I know I'm not the perfect one

nor will I ever be

I try to do the best I can

so my parents are proud of me

I know they love me; they told me so;

each and every night

They both give me a hug and kiss

and then turn out the light

I fall to sleep and dream about

how lucky I really am

for the mom and dad God gave to me

under his loving outstretched hands

MIRACLES

An event unconjurable to the mind of man

unexplainable by "Mother Nature's" laws

alienated from the pragmatism of scientific logic

These happenings or events have no magnitudes

within the realm of time

Understood by a deity far greater than oneself

So let us now be forever grateful

for all that we did have; now have; and could have

for true miracles do happen every day called life

LIFE'S MEANINGS

Life: A short period of time on earth

Life: Full of happiness and pain

Life: A book of memories to keep forever

Life: A steppingstone to eternal life

Life: Hell on earth

Life: Family and friends

Life: Full of riches

Life: Full of love and hate

Life: The giving of oneself to others

Life: It's worth all of this

Life's meanings are many

Its outcome you'll choose

DREAMING

We dream about life's yesterdays

and those that are to come

When awakening from our world of dreams

a new day has now begun

The truth be told to all mankind

to search is not to find

for within thyself the answer lies

It's been there all the time

So look upon the sky of blue

and the twinkling stars at night

for in your heart and soul to find

this search for eternal life

JOHN D. SCHMITZ

LIFE'S PAGES

Twilight opens the evening sky

The sun is fast to sleep

Another page in my book of life

that's committed to my memory

The moon and stars will guide me through

awaiting the break of dawn

With this new day; I'm happy to say

it's time to be moving on

I'll hop in my car; whatever purpose shall there be

just fill to my heart's content

these pages of life; as I see them unfold

to my memory is where they are sent

PAPA'S SHORT VERSES

1)   This word has but one meaning
       It destroys you day by day
       Left in its path the ruin of love
       and your hope for a better day

2)   Reality seems not so simple
       It perplexes the average man
       A mind to which will contemplate
       yet never understand

3)   Love is a many splendid thing
       as wide as a countryside
       small as a kiss upon one's lips
       or a tear that never dries

JOHN D. SCHMITZ

PAPA'S ONE LINERS

1)   Memories are like fish in the sea

        Once you catch one you'll never forget

2)   I gave it all I had

        My tank is empty

        No wonder you got nowhere

3)   I ran around the block a couple of times

        It really felt good; until I stopped

4)   Better now than later

        Don't tell that to Custer

5)   If at first you don't succeed

        try; try; again

        What should I do after that?

6)   Swimming is like a ballet in motion

        if you know how to swim

7)   I'll give you a hand

        as long as it's not mine

THE END   HA!! HA!! OH BOY